A HISTORY OF WORLD WAR TWO
told in letters, stories of romance, and vintage photos

by Barbara Storm Farr

Old Barn Publishing
WWW.OBEPUB.COM
Old Barn Enterprises, Inc.

A History of World War Two told in letters, stories of romance, and vintage photos by Barbara Storm Farr

Copyright © 2011 by Barbara Storm Farr (text) and William Farr (letters, captions, and photos). All rights reserved.

ISBN: 978-1-879009-33-2

No part of this book may be reproduced or transmitted in any form or by any means, electronic or mechanical, including photocopying, recording, or by any information storage and retrieval system, except where permission is specifically granted without the express written permission of the publisher.

To contact the author or publisher, visit www.obepub.com.

Disclaimer

Although the author and publisher have made every effort to ensure the completeness and accuracy of this book, we assume no responsibility for omissions, inaccuracies, or inconsistencies that may appear. Any perceived slights of people or organizations are unintentional. To the extent that this book provides recommendations or comparisons, they represent only the opinions of the author.

This book is sold with the understanding that neither the author nor the publisher are engaged in rendering professional advice. If expert assistance is required, the reader should consult with a competent professional.

The author and the publisher shall have neither liability nor responsibility to any person or entity with respect to any loss or damage caused, or alleged to be caused, directly or indirectly, by the information in this book.

Acknowledgements

Special thanks to Pam Farr for restoring the many vintage images shown in this book.

A HISTORY OF WORLD WAR TWO

told in letters, stories of romance,
and vintage photos

by Barbara Storm Farr

Introduction

Dear reader,

In words there is power. In stories there is insight. In shared experiences there is wisdom.

You'll find all of these qualities in this book.

And whether you're reading this in the 2000s or the 3000s, I think you'll find the stories told here — timeless.

I hope you will explore this book carefully, it is designed to be enjoyed on many levels — to amuse... give you insights...tell the story of a war...to touch your heart. But most of all, I hope you will notice one important thing — the power of letters.

In this book, you'll find many excerpts of letters written by my father. All carefully selected and put in their proper historical context by the author – my mother – who tells you the complete story.

The letters are still fresh as the day they were written. And they have a "presence" unmatched by any other type of communication. Take note of this.

The lesson? Let's not forget to use the power of personal one-on-one written communication in our own lives. After all, look what it did for me. As you will learn, without the letters in this book, and the relationship they created, *I* would not exist!

Yes, please do use this book as an inspiration to write and document your own personal story. Life itself, is a series of stories — do not let them be lost!

J FARR

Jeff Farr, son of William and Barbara Farr

Bill Farr's desk in San Severo, Italy, April 23, 1945 where many of the letters in this book were written.

"My Dear Miss Storm — or may I call you Barbara" began the first letter to me from PFC William Farr, Esler Field, Louisiana, dated December 14, 1943. My friend, George Dattilo, met Bill in the service, showed him my picture and encouraged him to begin a correspondence. This was the depth of the World War II years, and the many young men who were ripped from their homes, jobs, schools and families to defend their country were lonely for companionship if only through letter-writing. It was their only tie with the reality of home life before the war began and to which they longed to return. The women at home, lonely, too, for all the men were scattered at military locations throughout the world in conflict, maintained connections with the men in service. It was the patriotic thing to do! Thus PFC William Farr of the Army Air Corps and Barbara Storm, high school senior in Arlington Heights Township High School, Illinois, became acquainted through correspondence, developed a relationship, ultimately married and committed themselves to a lifetime together.

Bill Farr was a keen observer of his life as an enlisted man in the United States Army Air Corps during World War II. During 1944 and 1945 he wrote often, as many as four times a week from overseas. His letters describe the experiences that many young men like him endured during the war, and these letters have been preserved. Bill's impressions of people, military life on the army bases and war-ravaged Italy provide an important historical document of the war years. Most importantly, the letters convey Bill's feelings, opinions and thoughts during those uncertain times and his hopes and plans for the future. They were not unlike many of the men in service. These attitudes and individual plans of all the returning men after the war would formulate and build the "post-war" world of a new America.

Selections from Bill's letters form the nucleus of this book which chronicles the beginning of our personal relationship, the crucial years of the war in the Italian theater, the end of war and the beginning of peace time as seen through Bill's letters to me and my perspectives from the home front within the context of historical events.

World War II began in Europe on September 3, 1939, when Britain and France declared war on Germany in response to Germany's attack and invasion of Poland. Although the United States supported the Allies with supplies and munitions through the Lend Lease Act of early 1941, America was not actively involved until December 7, 1941, when Japan attacked Pearl Harbor, Honolulu, Hawaii, a U.S. Territory, devastating the American Pacific Fleet. President Franklin Roosevelt avowed this would be a "day which will live in infamy," and on December 8 the Congress declared a state of war with Japan. This momentous action was broadcast (live) to the nation on the radio. As a sophomore in high school, I remember well the entire student population of 500 being assembled in the gymnasium to hear the declaration. We sat quietly with fear and wonder of what the future held for the young people in that room. Some would be fired with the urgency to "join up" at the age of seventeen to defend their country. Others would be drafted on their eighteenth birthday and inducted even if they were in the middle of their senior year. Many would see action in the war, and many would not come back including one classmate who went down with one of the ships in the battle for Midway Island. Somehow we sensed, on that day in December, that our lives would never be the same and the rest of our high school days would not be carefree. On December 11 Germany and Italy, supporting their Tripartite partner, Japan, declared war on the United States plunging the nations of the world into total conflagration.

Bill Farr, who graduated from high school in June, 1941, worked a daytime job and in the evening attended Cooper Union School for the Advancement of Science and Art in New York City as a scholarship student. He was not eager to become part of the military, but when the "Greetings" notice from Selective Service arrived, he was resignedly inducted into the Army Air Corps on January 28, 1943. In his second, undated (approximately January, 1944) letter from Keesler Field, Mississippi, he described his army occupation:

> "Most of my army career has been spent doing photography. At Lowry Field, Denver, I got my schooling for photography. From there I was sent to the photo lab at Esler Field. As most other soldiers I wanted to keep moving, so I applied for aviation cadet training. After many months of waiting, I have finally been sent down here to take many tests. More than half are eliminated here, so I'll just hope and keep my fingers crossed."

Bill Farr at Lowry Field 1943

Bill Farr at Esler Field November 1943

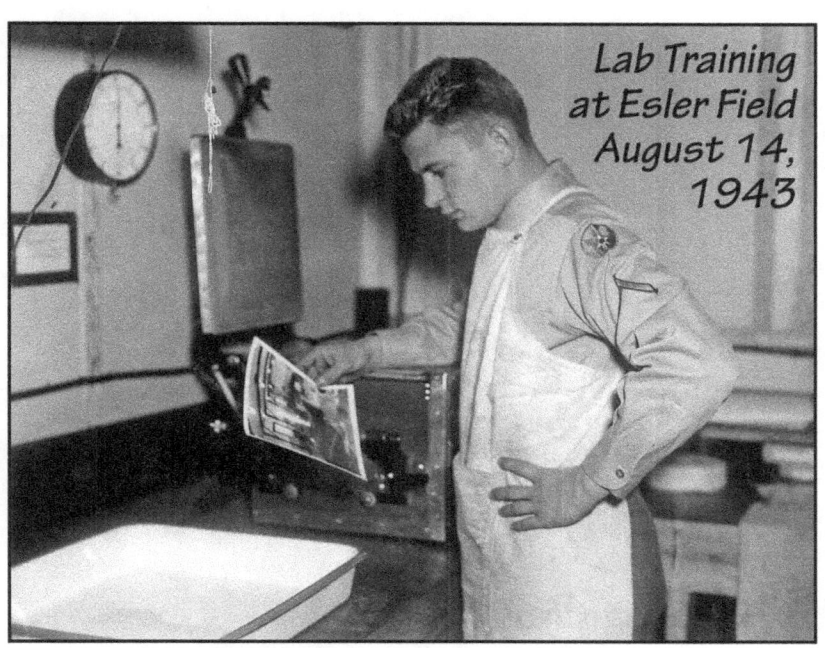

Lab Training at Esler Field August 14, 1943

Cadet training was not to be Bill's destiny, and perhaps he was fortunate, for air casualties mounted as the war progressed. In his letter of February 2, a prophetic date as we would be married just two years later, he wrote:

> *"This week my last hopes of making cadet were washed away... That made me feel pretty bad, but there just isn't a thing I can do. I know everything will eventually come out for the very best."*

Bill's fears that he would not be accepted for pilot training were confirmed. He wrote on February 13:

> *"As I expected, my name was on the wrong list. Even though I knew it was coming, it was hard to take. I had hopes of becoming a gunner-photographer, but now I've even been disqualified from gunnery school [one eye was not correctable to 20/20 vision]. Gee, I wanted to fly so bad, but if it's God's will that I stay on the ground it's OK with me."*

By April, 1944, Bill had been sent to Will Rogers Field, Oklahoma, for training in photo reconnaissance.

"This picture of me was taken by Bob Fieldle while I wasn't looking."

He described the purpose of the squadron in his April 5 letter:

> "An outfit of this kind is mainly responsible for getting pictures of enemy objectives which have been or are to be bombed. Pictures are also taken frequently to trace the movement of enemy forces. These pictures are in most part taken with the P-38 which is a two motored pursuit ship. The job of the photo department is to deliver the finished pictures to photo intelligence in as short a time as possible. When the plane with the pictures lands, a photo man is waiting to unload the film from the aerial camera. The film is rushed to the lab. It is then developed and dried which may take anywhere from 20 minutes to one hour, depending upon the length of the roll. The roll is now taken to the drafting department where only the good negatives are lettered. Now the film is brought into the printing room. After being printed the prints are washed, dried and sorted. That completes our job. Here the work is made a little more convenient with all the modern machinery we have. When in combat we'll probably work in the photo trailer. That's when things start getting rough."

P-38 Reconnaissance

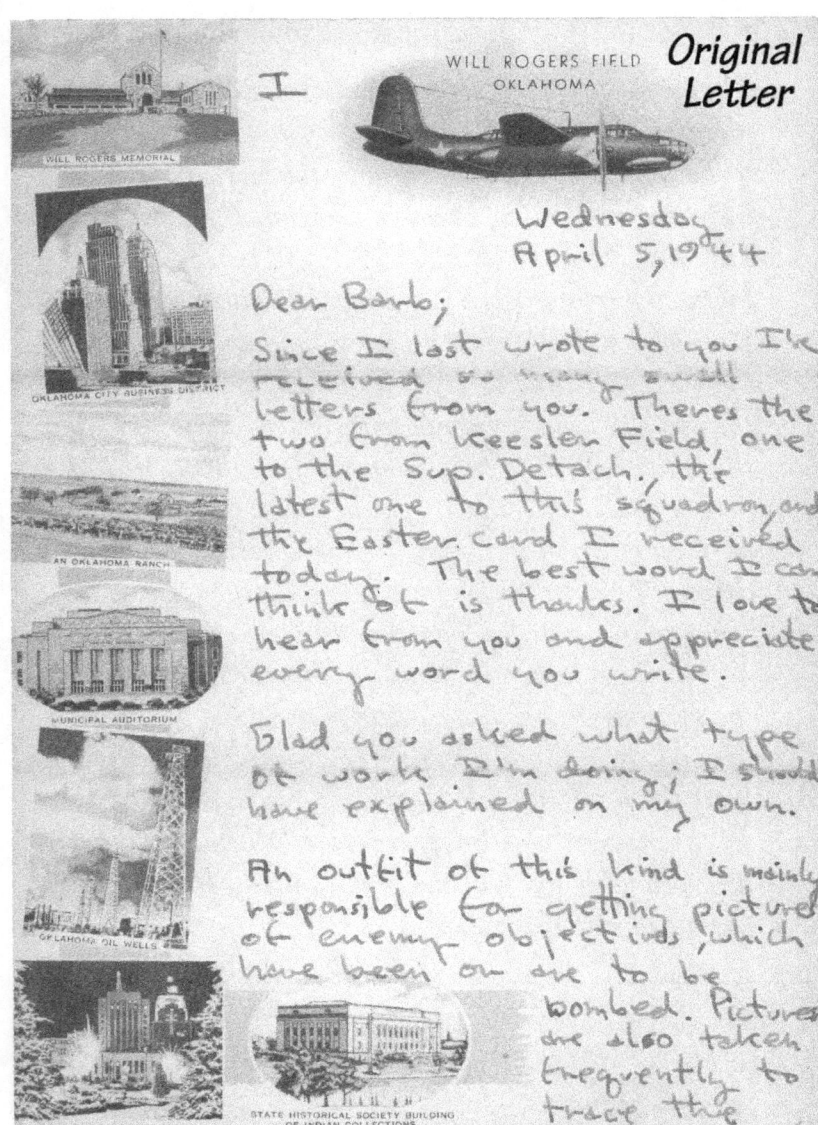

Original Letter

Wednesday
April 5, 1944

Dear Barb;

Since I last wrote to you I've received so many swell letters from you. Theres the two from Keesler Field, one to the Sup. Detach., the latest one to this squadron, and the Easter card I received today. The best word I can think of is thanks. I love to hear from you and appreciate every word you write.

Glad you asked what type of work I'm doing; I should have explained on my own.

An outfit of this kind is mainly responsible for getting pictures of enemy objectives, which have been or are to be bombed. Pictures are also taken frequently to trace the

Despite his inability to become a combat pilot, Bill found the opportunity to ride in some of the planes at Will Rogers Field by signing on as a temporary crew member. He went up in a C-78 as an engineer: *"That pilot really gave me a [one hour] ride I won't forget fast. He just returned from over-seas duty."* This was followed by a two hour ride in a B-25. These were practice flights for pilots either on rotation or about to be sent overseas for active duty.

By May, 1944, Bill was transferred again. His next letter, May 24, was from the 37 Photo Reconnaissance Squadron at the Muskogee Army Air Corps base in Oklahoma. This was a newly created squadron which was preparing to go overseas in the near future. The soldiers worked long hours, so they were especially grateful when the local population welcomed them. Bill recounts one episode:

> *"Last Sunday three of us were made to feel good. We went to the First Baptist Church in Muskogee [seven miles from the base]. The moment we walked into the church we were greeted and really felt welcome. After the service we were invited downstairs to enjoy a really delicious dinner. Surprising, because soldiers aren't usually welcomed like that here in the south.... That makes a fellow think he's really fighting for something."*

In June, 1944, Bill wrote from the base hospital where he had been a patient for two weeks as the result of an accident. This incident, though devastating, had a positive effect as the soldier with whom Bill collided during a baseball game became a life-long friend, Bill Groethe of Rapid City, South Dakota.

With friend Bill Groethe

Unfortunately, the medical care which Bill received was far from adequate, and the hemorrhaging from his cut lip and broken teeth required several blood transfusions. He recovered soon, however, or at least the Army decided he was able, for by July he was working twelve hours per day in an accelerated training program. He wrote:

> "Those black canvas labs we work in are the hottest things imaginable. I'm afraid to think what they're like in a tropic region [he expected to be sent to New Guinea]. Without a refrigeration system the

> *temperature of the developer goes up as high as 96 degrees."*

Obviously, the squadron was getting close to shipping out and army procedures were intensified. Bill related a thirty mile hike and overnight bivouac:

> *"We started out yesterday noon with our full field packs and rifles. At a quarter to six we arrived at the bivouac area. By one AM Sunday morning we were again on the way and got back to camp at about 7:15. All this week we'll be out on the range firing then next Saturday we go out on maneuvers."*

The bivouac was merely a warm-up for the next exercise described in an August 10, 1944 letter:

> *"Life here is pretty rough [after being in the wilderness for two weeks]. We live in five man tents. I've been bitten by everything, mosquitoes, chiggers, ants, spiders, etc. Chiggers are strange things. In fact. I've never seen one yet. They tell me they're little red bugs about the size of a pin point.... We use the old faithful mess kits and of course share the food with the ants by sitting on the ground."*

Bill concluded his letter by remarking that *"it's just about time to head for work again. So I'll put on my pistol belt, canteen, gas mask, rifle and steel helmet. I've tried to convince them that there aren't any Japs around, but they still insist we wear all our equipment."*

On Bivouac in Okmulgea Oklahoma
July and August 1944

Bill was anxious, as most of the service men were, to go overseas, and "get this war over." The war, which seemed to stretch endlessly, had finally turned in the direction of an Allied win. Even news commentators, such as Drew Pearson, were predicting that the war in Europe would be over by September 15, 1944, as Bill noted in his letter of July 23, 1944. This, however, was overly optimistic. The war would last many more months and incur many more casualties in both the European and Pacific theaters.

D-Day, June 6, 1944, the Allied invasion of Normandy, thrust the ground war back onto the European continent. Germany had dominated the English Channel, France, Belgium, the Netherlands, Poland, Czechoslovakia, Austria, Hungary, Roumania, Bulgaria, Yugoslavia, Norway, and Greece since the evacuation of British troops from Europe at Dunkirk, June 4, 1940. Four years of bitter war ensued. The Battle of Britain—a German blitzkrieg of bombing attacks—devastated the country. Major buildings in London still contain the pockmarks of the intensive shelling, and nearly one in five homes was destroyed or damaged. German U-Boats sank many British ships, limiting the effect of the British navy, but the sinking of Germany's giant battleship, the *Bismarck*, on May 27, 1940, and the diversion of German aircraft preparing to attack Russia in early 1941, saved Britain from invasion. With the European continent occupied or controlled by the Axis powers, Germany and Italy, the theater of war shifted to North Africa and the European colonial possessions.

As a result of nineteenth century explorations, conquests and national thrusts for empire, Africa was carved into possessions, colonies and protectorates by the major European nations—Belgium, Spain, Portugal, France, Great Britain, Germany and Italy. It was inevitable that interests would collide. Italy had, as recently as 1935, attacked and occupied Ethiopia which, along with previously acquired colonies of Libya, Eritrea and Somaliland, became Italian East Africa. At the beginning of the war, in September, 1940, Italy invaded British dominated Egypt. The British retaliated, pushing back the Italians and occupying all of Italian East Africa by the end of 1941. However, the

Germans under the direction of General Erwin Rommel, reinforced the Italians by attacking the British in the deserts of Libya and pushing them back to the Egyptian border. Some of the most intense fighting of the war took place on these sun-parched sand dunes of North Africa. Not until November 12, 1942, did the British army prevail and expel Rommel's army from Egypt after the battle of El Alamein.

A combined Anglo-American army invaded French Morocco and Algeria which was then administered by the Vichy (France) government under the domination of Germany. By May, 1943, Germany and Italy had retreated. Britain and the United States possessed the entire North African coast while Egypt and the Suez Canal remained under British domination. The Allies were positioned to begin an invasion of Italy. This would occur in July, 1943. General Patton led 250,000 British and American troops over the beachheads and across the belly of Sicily into Palermo. Italian officers, reflecting a war-weary populace, urged King Victor Emmanuel III to negotiate peace with the Allies. Mussolini, Il Duce, Dictator and Prime Minister, had lost favor and prestige with his fellow fascists as well as with most Italians. On July 25 the King, at the urging of the Grand Council of Fascists removed Mussolini from office and ordered him arrested. Meanwhile, General Mark Clark and the Allied Fifth Army landed at Salerno, just below Naples on the mainland. The Allies expected a quick victory. They were surprised. German tanks, planes and troops had been rushed in to thwart the Allied advance. Fighting was intense during the winter of 1943-44 through rugged terrain, mud and deplorable conditions. The road to Rome from Naples, 100 miles, took eight hard-fought months, culminating in the liberation of Rome on June 4, 1944, just two days before the Allied invasion of Normandy.

Germany's vigorous defense of Italy was somewhat unexpected by the Allies as Germany was fiercely occupied on the Eastern Front. Germany had invaded Russia, her former non-aggression pact partner, on June 22, 1941. The Russians were ill-prepared and the German army sowed paths of destruction through Russia. With much sacrifice the Russians defended the Germans' siege of Leningrad for seventeen months. This was followed by the battle for Stalingrad in February, 1943, which historian Norman Davies described as the "largest single battle of world history." One million men were killed. The Soviets pushed the German armies back, aided by American assistance with one billion tons of foodstuffs, 6500 planes, and 138,000 motor vehicles. By the middle of 1944 the Soviets had reached the border of East Prussia. The long-awaited "Second Front," urged by Stalin to relieve the Eastern Front, diverted the Germans from Russia, but the war in Europe was far from over. The beaches of Normandy, the hedgerows of France and the rough terrain of Italy were strewn with the bodies of Americans and British.

The naval war in the Pacific during 1943-44 followed a pattern of "leap-frogging" from one to another furiously defended island by "fight to the death" Japanese: Tarawa, Bouganville, Eniwetok, the coast of New Guinea, the Marshalls. The casualties were enormous. Following the surprise attack on Pearl Harbor in December, 1941, the Japanese had forced the Americans from the Philippine Islands, a U.S. Possession since 1898, then quickly occupied the Netherlands East Indies (Celebes, New Ireland, the Solomons, Java), Singapore, Burma and part of New Guinea. Japan had drawn a huge circle around its homeland, occupying much of China and the Western Pacific. Moreover, Japan lay within striking distance of New Zealand and Australia where the Allied Commander, General Douglas MacArthur, had established headquarters. At great cost the Allies prevailed in the naval Battle of the Coral Sea for Midway Island (June, 1942), halting Japan's eastward expansion. Shortly afterwards, August 7, U.S. Marines landed in the Solomon Islands, capturing Guadalcanal with heavy losses. Thus began a slow, costly, Allied drive to resist the Japanese occupiers of most of the Western Pacific islands.

By August 1, 1944, the Americans had prevailed in the Battle of the Philippine Sea, destroying 345 Japanese planes and three aircraft carriers. The main islands of the Marianas, Saipan, Tinian, Guam, were in American hands, but the major reconquest of the Philippines and the invasion of the Japanese homeland remained.

In the summer of 1944, life on the home front was in a state of suspended animation. Everyone longed for the end of the war, and each Allied successful battle was cheered, but we knew that victory was not yet in our grasp. In early June I graduated from high school with a high grade point average, but no possibility of attending college. Scholarships were scarce, and there was no money in my family to support me. My early ambition focused on becoming an airline stewardess, but first one must be a registered nurse. And that required three years of education! After a little investigation, I discovered that the Navy Nurse Corps recruited women for a period of four years, providing all the training with the expectation that graduates would serve in the Navy for at least a period of one year. However, the minimum age was nineteen, and as a fresh high school graduate, I was only seventeen. There was only one solution: take a job and wait. Perhaps the war would last long enough for me to join the Navy.

During the summer after my junior year, I was employed by the Eastman Kodak retail store in downtown Chicago. Upon graduation, I was offered a permanent job as a clerk at the film counter for the quite satisfactory salary of $20 for a five and one half day week. Even with the expense of commuting by train from Mount Prospect each day, I managed to save a little money to buy some U.S. Bonds for the war effort. The days were long, and very busy. One day in early September, 1944, I received a surprise call. Bill Farr was in Chicago, passing through on his way back to Oklahoma after a furlough at his home in New Jersey. After writing letters to one another for nine months, he was determined to meet me face-to-face. Within the hour, he arrived at Eastman Kodak.

I still remember Bill standing across the store while I finished waiting on a customer. Of course, I recognized him from the pictures that he had sent to me. He looked even better in person! Dark blond hair, blue eyes, trim in his Army Air Corps uniform, Bill was a handsome young man of twenty. He had secured a room at the YMCA, but I, and my mother who also worked at Eastman Kodak, invited him to come to Mount Prospect and stay with us for the two nights that he would be in Chicago before returning to his air base. This was our "first date." We had dinner at Henrici's—a famous restaurant that no longer exists. We went to the movies, we saw a horrendous picture called "The Hairy Ape," with William Bendix (we still laugh about it!), we strolled through Grant Park and watched the colored lights playing on Buckingham Fountain. Bill presented me with a gift—a gold and silver compact. It was a bittersweet time, for just as we had become acquainted, we had to part. Bill knew that he was within weeks of going overseas—to where he had no idea. Perhaps he would return; perhaps he would be another war casualty. But we had met, had enjoyed a brief interlude of romance in an ugly world of death and destruction, and like many other young people, our lives would be determined by the course of the war.

Barbara Storm Farr at Buckingham Fountain

Bill's next letter from Muskogee, Oklahoma was dated September 17, 1944: *"It's really hard coming back to a place like this after spending three of the most wonderful days of my life with you."* Our brief meeting had made an indelible impression on both of us, and, suddenly, for Bill, I was the "girl back home" that was in every service man's dream. As yet he had no word of whether his squadron would be sent to the European or Pacific theaters or when.

Bill Farr at Muskogee A.F.B. 1944

Bill Farr with Jeep at Muskogee, A.F.B. Oklahoma September, 1944

Despite the uncertainty of the future, Bill was planning ahead. He had obtained catalogs of numerous colleges to pursue at the war's end, and he had started a correspondence course in Algebra. He looked to the future with optimism:

> *"With more hopes and more ambitions, our country may once again prosper as it should. There are just too many men who say they don't know what to do or have nothing to go back to civilian life for, so they say. I am not one of those. That's why I'm one of the luckiest men on earth. I do have something to come back to and live for. That's right, isn't it?"*

Action in the squadron at Muskogee Air Field had slowed.

Apparently, the orders to move overseas were delayed by the stalemates on the frontlines, both in the European and Pacific theaters. Much of Bill's time was spent watching training films and listening to lectures. He characterized the situation in a letter of September 20: *"I hope something happens soon because I don't like the way things are right now. Kill time and time will kill you."* The squadron kept the men abreast of the fighting fronts on a giant world map, and Bill noted that the Japanese were sweeping across China.

Waiting to join the war...

"Our lack of interest in that theater is a big mistake, I think. Japan is the American people's real enemy.... Each Japanese gain in China will eventually mean that more American boys and more American war material will have to be used that would otherwise have been the case."

Apparently, Bill and his fellow soldiers also spent much time in discussion, especially concerning politics. The General Election for the President and the Congress would be held in November and Bill had some very definite views:

> *"I am happy to report that we Dewey [Thomas Dewey of New York, Republican candidate for President] men are getting stronger every day....I am really quite confident that Dewey can and will win."*

Dewey lost. President Franklin Roosevelt won an unprecedented fourth term in office. Although it was rumored that he was in ill health and might not live long enough to fulfill his term, the American electorate was reluctant to change leadership in the middle of a war. Bill's excursion into Republican politics was destined to be brief. By the end of the war and his return to civilian life, Bill would support the leftist Progressive Party headed by Henry Wallace and eventually become a Democrat. But that is another story.

Writing on September 30, 1944, Bill noted that *"the war has certainly slowed down."* Germans were resisting on all fronts, and the war was now expected to last at least into 1945 in Europe and probably two years longer to defeat Japan. The squadron was close to shipping out and Bill confided: *"Took my last trip to town [Muskogee, OK] this afternoon. Starting tomorrow morning we're restricted to the base awaiting orders. This is just between you and me."* As we both knew, *"loose lips sink ships."*

On October 2, Bill reported:

> *"Yesterday we rushed around like mad from morning to night. While the church service was being held*

we were in hearing the Articles of War read to us. When we were through with that, we returned to the barracks for a G.I. party. A G.I. party is the term given for the time when everyone has to scrub the barrack. We did exactly that. Cleaned the windows, scrubbed the floors, and dusted everything in sight."

The next few letters were from *"somewhere on the East Coast"* waiting for shipping orders. On October 12, he commented:

"The way the war stands now it is possible for us to be sent to any part of the world. It does look as though the Germans will fight to the very end. Maybe it is best to fight it out this time; after all this is only a continuance of what is called world war one. I'd be willing to sacrifice anything to spare the next generation the horrors of war."

His last letter from the States, dated October 16, complained:

"Finally you feel that you're headed for a place where the training you've gotten will be put to use and you'll finally be able to contribute to the war effort. What happens then? They leave you lay around doing all kinds of unpleasant details [K.P. duty]"

Sgt. Dinehart Learns KP...

...looks like he's got it!

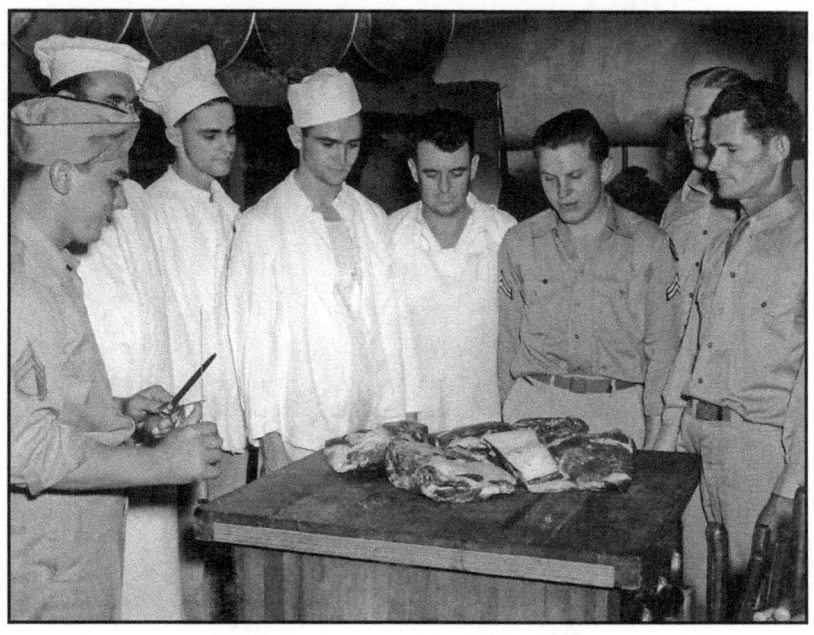

Shortly thereafter, the squadron shipped out. Bill sailed from Newport News, Virginia, on the second to last troop ship of a 100 ship convoy of Liberty ships and destroyers. The trip across the Atlantic would take thirty days. German U-Boats would pick off the last ship and sink it. Bill would relate years later the sick feeling of watching that ship go down, knowing that the convoy could not stop to pick up survivors, and not knowing if that U-Boat would be back to sink another ship. The convoy reached the Straits of Gibraltar, split for various ports, and the lone ship that carried Bill sailed on to Naples, Italy.

Naples, Italy, March 15, 1945
"From this harbor I got my first look at Italy. We docked at the far right."

By November, 1944, Naples had been occupied by U.S. forces for one year. Italy had surrendered unconditionally on September 3, 1943, followed by the rescue of Mussolini on September 12 by a German glider troop. Mussolini fled to the north of Italy and gathered his remaining supporters into a Republican Fascist Party in alliance with the occupying German Army. A civil war ensued of anti-Fascist Italians against the Mussolini Fascists and the Germans. Despite this conflict, the Germans maintained control of Rome until June, 1944. The Allies expected to use the airfields around Rome as bases to bomb southern Germany while ground troops pressed into northern Italy and quickly destroyed the German forces led by Field Marshal Kesselring. This might have been possible if the British and Americans had agreed upon military strategy. Unfortunately, for the Italian campaign, the agreement hammered out by British Prime Minister Winston Churchill, United States President Franklin Roosevelt and Premier Josef Stalin of the Soviet Union at the Teheran Conference in November, 1943, now became contentious.

At the Teheran Conference, the Allied Powers agreed that the primary military goal should focus on "Overlord," the invasion of Normandy. Meanwhile the British and American land troops would push up opposite sides of the Italian peninsula. At the same time an Allied amphibious landing on the French Riviera, named "Anvil," would divert German divisions and allow the Normandy invasion to proceed across France to Germany. All of these plans depended upon the capture of Rome which did not occur until two days before D-Day. Germany sent more divisions into Italy and stopped the Allies just north of Florence.

The Germans stood firm at a line across Italy, the "Gothic Line," from Spezzia on the Gulf of Genoa to Rimini on the Adriatic Sea. The ground war was stalemated while the Allies' attention was diverted to the invasion of Normandy and the projected landing on the French Riviera.

Churchill claimed that operation Anvil, now renamed "Dragoon," was poor strategy. He wanted to amass Army divisions in Italy, drive the Germans north to Vienna and open up a back door to Germany. Despite many communications between Churchill and President Roosevelt, the Americans were unbending. Supreme Allied Commander General Dwight Eisenhower was determined to balance the Normandy invasion with the southern French landing on August 15 and thrust those armies north through France to Strasburg. As Churchill claimed in his chronicle, *The Second World War, Volume Six, Triumph and Tragedy*, the withdrawal of Allied divisions from Italy prolonged the war. The Germans poured troops into northern Italy, but not into southern France, so that the Riviera invasion met little resistance and did not fulfill its mission to divert the Germans from Normandy. As a result the war in Italy would drag on until the following spring. Action in Italy during the winter of 1944-45 depended primarily on bombers and fighter planes of the Army Air Corps and Britain operating from air fields in the south.

The next communication from Bill was a V...-Mail dated November 24, 1944. (V, standing for Victory, followed by the Morse code for "V." As a space-saver, letters were written on a form, photographed, and the film transported back to the United States. The resulting photograph, 4 x 5 inches, was sent to the addressee after being read and approved by the official censor.) Bill was "somewhere in Italy" (which I would learn later was San Severo twenty-five miles from the Adriatic Coast), writing by candlelight in a structure that had no heat.

However, the Army had provided a decent Thanksgiving Day dinner the day before and Bill was "holding up all right" even though "living has been pretty much in the rough...." In his next letter, November 26, he described the conditions he encountered:

> *"Being over here really gives one the opportunity to see the ravages of war. It's really more horrible than one can imagine not seeing it. Most are simply dressed in rags. The filth is terrific. Above all I feel so sorry for the children....Most of them are barefoot. It appears as though some of them have not been washed for weeks or maybe months. The dirt is just crusted on their feet, hands and back of the neck. Most of them are very nice and intelligent....*
>
> *Cigarettes and soap can be used for money. They pay as much as five dollars for a carton of cigarettes. It's really amazing to see five and six year olds going around inhaling cigarettes. We've made friends with some of the children near our place, so if possible, we're planning to take them a few things for Christmas."*

San Severo Italy, 1945

"This is not an uncommon site at all. Many people have chicken, pigs and so forth right in their homes"

The next night, on guard duty, Bill wrote another letter by candlelight in which described the town where he was stationed:

> *"Most of the places we've lived in were undoubtedly beautiful homes at one time. Due to the war they are pretty run down....Even in their houses they the [Italians] show their love of art. All the floors have very intricate designs on them; the ceilings even more so. The room I now live in has about an 18 foot ceiling. It has on it many paintings of angels, flowers, fruit horns, and other typical Italian art. Even in the largest homes there is a lack of toilet and heating facilities. I still haven't seen a shower or bathtub in any home.*

The streets are mostly overgrown alley ways. Cars are just about extinct. The roads are usually full of horse and mule driven carts. Many of the people live right in the same room with the animals. The filth is really sickening at times. My drinking friends like this place because there is plenty of vino which is Italian for wine. A whole quart can be gotten for a bar of chocolate or a pack of cigarettes."

Bill and another soldier spent some free time walking around the small town, and he related his impressions:

"All of these towns are just full of churches. There must be about one for every few hundred people. Inside, all of them are extremely elaborate. Many of the fixtures seem to be made of solid gold and probably are.... If that money was used properly it could afford these people a new clean way of life....Also saw a strange funeral procession. Leading were a number of children all dressed alike. Beside them were the mothers trying to keep them in line. Following them were the padres or priests with their colorful costumes. Then came the hearse and behind it a brass band. I suppose being over here and seeing the world is an education in itself. I hope I don't become too well educated!"

Photo shown below... Italy, February 1945. **Caption on back...** *"One of the better looking court yards. The Sunday carriage is on the left and the stable is on the right behind it. The street is very narrow and dingy, so it is really surprising to see something so picturesque upon entering. Note how everything is arched. This is done for strength since wood or steel is not available."*

The town was shared with many English soldiers, and Bill was not impressed with their attitudes:

> "I can't help disliking them. They won't speak to you because they think they're so much superior to us. What gripes me most of all is the fact they won't even pick us up in the trucks that we've given to them. [American Lend-Lease provided much materiel, including trucks, to Britain.]"

Sanitation remained a problem, so Bill wrote:

> "Believe it or not I have one of the world's worst hair cuts—a G.I. Over here it is almost impossible for one to keep real clean at times. Most times we have to use our helmets for sinks. That is really a wonderful piece of equipment."

Bill did not write any letters for one month. On December 20, 1944, he described his inability to write: *"It's been this unsettled feeling with everything and everyone in a turmoil."* The men had been issued tents, and it was up to the occupants to make them comfortable. There were no floors, and rain fell incessantly:

> "Once it starts raining, it lasts for days. Then comes mud such as I've never seen before. There have been days when the mud has come above and then inside my high shoes. The rainy season is soon to start. That is another reason we're all so anxious to get under cover for good."

Bill and his five tent mates secured enough brick for the floor, which they laid in their spare time. However, they were planning to build a *"grande casa"* (grand house) for themselves in the olive grove.

> *"We had to obtain our material by taking down a deserted Italian "casa" and then hauling it to our camp in the dark."*

The men also took sandblocks for the walls, and hired some Italians to put the structure together. With chocolate and cigarettes as barter, a very nice little house was under construction.

Construction of the Grande Casa in the Olive grove, San Severo Italy, 1945

Christmas Day, 1944, a cold one in Italy, found a melancholy Bill writing and longing to be home again. He felt very sad that the Italian children were running about in rags with bare feet in a town devoid of any Christmas decoration or spirit. Yet the children were playing and laughing!

> *"The whole town itself looked very normal. The only sign of Christmas was the excessive ringing of all the church bells. The war itself didn't stop either. All day the planes flew over as usual."*

Despite the uncertainty of the future and the slow progress of the war, Bill was optimistic at the beginning of 1945:

> *"In this new tomorrow lies hope, hope for the peace which will bring us all back home to our loved ones.*

Looking back on the old year, I can see many beautifully lighted spots. The wonderful days with you and even some lonely hours just thinking of you, some of my G.I. friends who have afforded me good companionship, and all that just living has taught me."

Bill also started the New Year with a new friend: a black puppy one month old which he named Smudgepot. He bought him from an Italian for four packs of cigarettes.

This was not Bill's first dog since he entered the Air Corps. While at Muskogee, Oklahoma in August, 1944, Bill had written:

"You should see the three sweet little puppies we have in our tent. We found them in a paper bag out on the road. When we found them they were pretty lifeless, but are now coming along fine. We'll take them back to camp and raise them."

Bill adopted one of the pups and named him "Burma." Unfortunately, in October, Burma disappeared from the Base. Bill surmised that someone had stolen him, but Bill would have had to leave the dog very shortly as he shipped out of Muskogee, Oklahoma a few weeks later.

Bill Farr and Burma

Owning a dog lent some warmth into Bill's life in the cold, wet winter of Italy in 1945:

> *"For days we had nothing but rain. That resulted in mud, mud and more mud. This mud is worse than slushy snow to get around in. It's more slippery, deeper in most places and of course dirtier if you fall down in it, which is not an unrare occurrence. Two nights ago I was on guard duty. It started to hail. I had on just about all the clothes I own and was still cold. It's the type of cold which is damp and seeps through anything....While crossing a huge muddied area some days ago I slipped and fell on my back. My buddy who was with me laughed and all I could do was laugh too. Actually, it wasn't funny at all. I must have gained a hundred pounds or so with all the mud hanging on me."*

Construction of the house occupied almost all of Bill's spare time. He described their means of heating:

> *"The stoves are all made by our squadron welders from old drums, gas cans or whatever is available. Gasoline is used, and is gravity fed from a tank outside the tent. The stove pipe is the hardest thing to get. Ours is made of some old sheet metal we found along the road. We took it to a tinsmith in town and he really did a nice neat job on it."*

In addition to a stove, the new house had a fireplace:

> *"It's built around the 50 gallon gasoline drum stove we made. The chimney is made of brick, and has*

a flashy looking spark arrester of brick on top. The whole thing works beautifully."

However, the house was still not livable, and the men remained in their tent:

"Although we've practically worked on the house until twelve every single night, it still isn't finished. The big hold up is the water proofing for the roof. We have a huge pile of curved tile piled up on a lot. Up till now the weather has been so bad that a truck cannot be gotten to it."

"Here is where we draw our rations each week." San Severo, Italy, March 1945

Building the house, though important to the men's comfort, was a diversion from the actual daily routine of establishing a photo laboratory to produce the pictures taken by the reconnaissance planes flying over enemy territory.

Bill's attention was ever on the progress of the war. On January 12, 1945 he observed:

> *"Last night I heard the news of MacArthur's landings on Luzon in the Philippines. That must be a great day for him. Already they have penetrated some twenty miles inland. By the looks of the situation now, I think the finish of the European and Asiatic campaigns may be a close tie. That's what I'm hoping for anyway. I don't relish the idea of moving to another theater of operations and going through this same stage."*

Always, the possibility of being diverted to the Pacific operation loomed over the men at San Severo. The loneliness, the uncertainty, the homesickness showed through Bill's lament:

> *"Right now, it seems but yesterday that I held you in my arms. Now I'm so far from you it's hard to realize."*

But Bill still was optimistic: *"The way time is passing it'll just be a tomorrow before I'm back. I'll be thinking of you always."*

The war in Italy was stalemated by weather. As Bill observed:

> *"The temperature is somewhere around freezing and it's hailing with a stingy wind blowing. On a night like this I just can't help but realize how fortunate I am to be in safety and a fairly warm place. Those boys are having a tough time fighting a war in this kind of weather. The whole Italian front is now covered*

with fourteen inches of snow and it's about 20 degrees below zero.... Everyone writes and asks how I like sunny Italy. I simply can't figure out what gives them the idea this place is sunny. I've seen less sun here than anywhere I've ever been."

On January 28 Bill had an interesting observation concerning the Russian's role in the war:

"As much as I want this war to end, I don't like to see the Russians do it themselves for that will only mean that they will expect to dictate the peace terms. That isn't good because contrary to popular belief, Russia is a power and land hungry nation. If Russia has too much to say in the peace, she will only give our present enemies more room for revenge and assure another war."

These were prophetic words, for there would be another war—a cold war between the Soviet Union and the western Allies lasting four decades after the end of World War II.

Meanwhile, the war in Italy continued through the cold, wet winter, but, at last, Bill reported that the sun shone. Writing on February 1, he rejoiced that *"Italy has earned its name of sunny. Even the Italians seemed to be in better spirits. Guess it's the beautiful real sunshine that got into everyone."* However, Bill deplored the situation in San Severo, a typical rural Italian community:

"One thing that's been holding up the Allies around here are the Italian donkey carts, which are always crowding the streets. So many of these people are primitive and live in a little world of their own. All

they ask for in life is a little home where they can come to and eat, drink wine and sleep. That too, is why they are so easily led. I also blame their backwardness and poverty almost directly to the church. That is where the people put their money and that is where it stays...."

Bill and his friends lived more comfortably than their comrades in the tents. The little house that they had built, which was a project in progress, was wired for electricity and they were building a shower:

"We can get the planes' belly gas tanks if they are dropped and damaged. We intend setting these tanks on top of the house. The water will of course be gravity fed. We even have plans for building hot water heat so we can have both hot and cold running water. Right now we're concentrating on building a wash basin in one corner of the shower room. We feel that it's quite an achievement having built such a nice place as this in our spare time..."

"How wonderful a feeling it is to see something like this go up and knowing that you have a share in it. I hope that someday I'll be able to build another house and have you share with me the joy in seeing it go up. Can't you imagine what fun it would be planning, picking a sight, and sometimes even wondering where the money for it will come? All those small things are life itself and the things that bring real, true happiness."

Standing Left to Right
"Your Bill", Laddie Gazik, Bill Groethe

Kneeling Left to Right
Ed Greer, "Smudge Pot", Dick Monit

San Severo, Italy
June, 1945

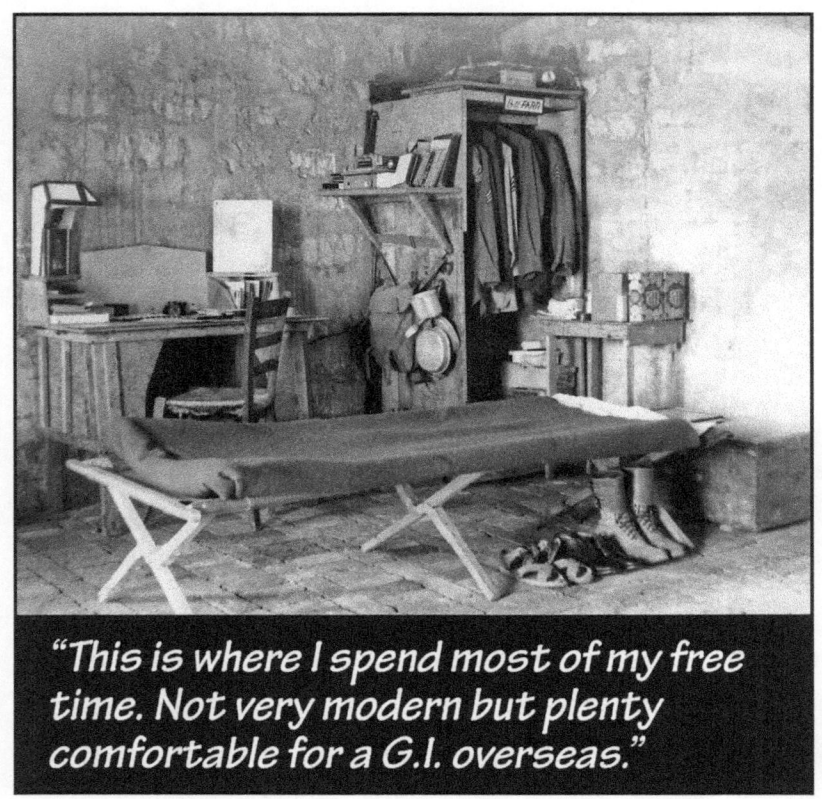

"This is where I spend most of my free time. Not very modern but plenty comfortable for a G.I. overseas."

Forty-five years would pass before Bill would fulfill his dream of designing and building a house, but the skills he learned building that little house in Italy enabled him to become an expert in the tools and concepts of construction.

Bill became acquainted with the Italian carpenter who had made a chair for him for six dollars. When Bill came to pick up the chair, he and the carpenter discussed politics:

> "The carpenter told us he was once in the Italian army, but was wounded at Palermo, Sicily, by an American bomb, and discharged. He claims he never believed in Mussolini, but could do nothing about

it. He said if they didn't work and keep their mouths shut, they wouldn't get their food rations. They'll all give you the same story. If enough people don't like someone they could always get rid of him. That goes for these Italian people too in regard to Mussolini. I can't have any sympathy at all for the grown up Italians for many of them who now walk the streets as free men shot and killed American boys. It seems all of them have intentions of going to America after the war. We told him not to try for we have too many already....

We tried to explain to the carpenter that if he started to do some real thinking for himself and spoke to all his country men, they too could form a Democratic government and in time derive from it all the advantages we in the good ole U.S. have. These people have just been under the control of a single person or power for so long that they just can't realize how strong a united people can be."

By the end of February the weather was warm and sunny. That increased the number of reconnaissance planes taking off to photograph enemy lines and more work for the photo laboratory. Bill commented that the "nice weather has kept us pretty busy, even working late nights quite often." He could not explain exactly what he was doing until the war ended, but in a later letter he described the situation:

"Being in an outfit such as I am gives me a chance at a great deal of information for we are in a position to see it all from above. Our photography showed the bombers where to bomb, told the infantry how much

> *opposition to expect, told headquarters how much damage bombs did, and made the last minute maps for which all invasions, drives, etc., were plotted. You see even though we've been way back here in comparative safety we have been doing an extremely important job."*

Indeed the Photo Reconnaissance operation played an important part in winning the war in Europe as saturation bombing by the Allies eventually overwhelmed the Germans, destroying, unfortunately, many beautiful cities and killing many civilians, but winning a final, total victory.

Despite his busy days, Bill was able to get some time off and visit a neighboring village, Foggia. In his February 22 letter he described his impressions:

> *"The first impression you get is that it is more war torn than the average town around here. The way the people live is enough to sicken a person. Most of the day was spent just walking around looking at all the shops. The Italian stores are all very small. Due to inflation all goods are tremendously high here and what they do have is of poor quality."*

Bill was so depressed by the conditions in Foggia that he took few photographs. *"It's sad enough remembering the poverty without having pictures of it."*

Wash Day in Foggia, February, 1945

The war continued, and Bill wondered at the Germans' perseverance:

> *"How and why the Germans keep on fighting is amazing. Almost every day and night the planes with their loads of death and destruction zoom overhead. This is a new type of war. It takes almost as many men far behind the lines in all types of vital jobs to keep the war going as it does on the front. Today with the long range planes of all types it is possible to be far from the front lines and still do the job without being harassed continually by the enemy.*
>
> *Best of all the news is that of the huge raid on Tokyo."*

After the Americans captured Saipan in the Marianas, and established air bases, B-29 Superfortress bombers began to inundate the Japanese islands with incendiary bombs. The battle for Iwo Jima, at the high cost of nearly 20,000 American lives, brought U.S. forces within 750 miles of Yokohama. Victory seemed inevitable, and as Bill observed:

> "We're getting there, thank God. It's very terrible, however, that so many lives must be lost and so many more hearts broken to achieve our goal of victory."

After many, miserable months Bill had become bitter and belligerent towards our capitulated enemy, Italy:

> "All these people are just as much responsible for the war and my being in their miserable country as the Germans. There is but one difference between the two, and that is the fact that the Italians just didn't have enough guts to fight the war to a finish. I'll never have any sympathy for these people since I know that so many who now walk the streets free men shot and killed American boys."

One very amusing incident described the attitude of the Italians:

> "One of the boys bought a souvenir handkerchief in a town near here. When he got back he held the item to the light for inspection. To his amazement he found that originally the handkerchief was made to sell to the Germans, for you could see the swastikas under the American tri colors which had been stenciled on after the Germans left."

Perhaps, today, we would call that entrepreneurship and clever recycling, but to Bill, the Italians were the enemy and one of the causes of the world's cataclysm. In retrospect it is difficult to understand how we all felt, whether on the front lines or on the home front, but those feelings of resentment, and indeed hatred, for the Axis nations who had plunged the world into a horrific war, were in response to the sacrifices we were all forced to make.

Italy, April 24, 1945 "No comments"

Every man in service longed to return home, to the "girl of his dreams" which he hoped would still be waiting for him. As the war in Europe seemed to be in its final stages, in February, 1945, Bill did some hard thinking about his future.

> *"I've been doing a lot of thinking lately, mostly about you and me and the peace which will bring me back home. Our love affair has been so very much different than others. I've known you quite a time yet haven't really had time enough with you to talk about many things. Those few wonderful days I spent with you kept me from reality and with little to say. I will never forget that last second when I put you in the taxi at the train station. Now here I am way over here with promises to you and have given you nothing to hold to.*
>
> *Someday soon, if you will accept it, I want to put a ring on your finger."*

Thus, in this manner, Bill proposed. Obviously, my response was positive, for Bill wrote in his letter of March 21, 1945: "Your answer to my question made me very happy. Such words will make all my time away from you more happy just knowing that you love me and will be waiting for me."

Part Two

WAR ENDS. ROMANCE CONTINUES.

Italy in the spring of 1945 lay impoverished, its people disunited. Italian Partisans in the north fought the Germans fiercely as well as attacking their fellow countrymen, the Republican Fascists who supported Mussolini, while the Allies occupied and controlled the South, Sicily, and Sardinia.

But to the common folk in the primitive villages bordering the Adriatic sea, life went on as it had for many centuries. Observing this culture, a new experience, Bill was intrigued and sought to document the rural Italians unique way of life.

Bill loved to take pictures. He was just beginning to realize that photography was a significant art form, and he set out to create images of the local people. The Italian villagers were drawn like magnets to soldiers with cameras:

> *"Everyone is kind to you when you have a camera. One man brought me a chair to sit on while I took a picture of his court yard. Another offered us wine. We went into a huge winery the owner of which spoke English pretty well. He showed us the whole process of wine making which was interesting. On the way back to camp, we passed the huge town cemetery. It is the most beautifully constructed and landscaped thing around. It seems that people are buried in accordance to their importance or the amount of money they can spend. For the town officials, huge elaborate vaults are built. The medium class is buried in marble tombs on the sides of huge long walls. The poorer people go 6 feet under."*

Cemeteries, in Italy as in most countries, revealed the stratification of society.

Bill received a much needed furlough in March, and he went to Naples. He wrote on March 21:

"Here I sit once again before the fireplace and under the light of a candle. That must sound like one of our American eras gone by.

> *The trip from camp to Naples was indeed a very beautiful one. Of course we were all on our own and had to hitch hike [with military vehicles]. Practically the whole way is through very mountainous country. There is a town about 40 miles east of Naples called Ariano Irpi. Its altitude must be at least 6000 or 7000 feet. There are a number of homes built on the edge of an 800 foot cliff which goes straight down. All Allied troops are forbidden to be in that town. Most of the people are still with the Axis, because they probably don't know much about the war. All they know is that we bombed their homes and churches so they don't like us.*
>
> *Naples is practically the same as any small town around here, except that all is on a much larger scale. More people, larger slum areas, bigger churches, more children pestering you, and many more stores selling all types of worthless over-priced souvenirs. The Red Cross occupies a very large beautiful building, probably a government building before the war. That is always the first place a fellow goes for information, something to eat, or maybe just to spend a few hours in a place with a bit of an American atmosphere.*
>
> *One day was spent in the ancient ruins of the city,*

Pompeii. It was surprising that their culture and manner of living did not seem to me to be much different than that of the present day Italians. The streets were just as narrow, the architecture is basically the same, with the typical open court yards and bathrooms built right into the kitchens. America is so new compared to this country, yet we are already so far ahead of them.

We had all intentions of climbing Mount Vesuvius, but it was stopped about a week ago when it erupted slightly and hurt a number of people who live up there.... I can't understand why people continue to build cities right next to a living volcano. There is always a possibility that it might erupt and again cover many homes."

"General Street Scene" Pompeii, March 14, 1945

"The temple of Jupiter in the fourth square!"
Pompeii, March 14, 1945

The scenery was beautiful, but Bill had harsh words for the Neapolitans he encountered:

> *"Wherever you go people are trying to sell or beg something of you. Nuns, priests, monks are always begging for money. At first all this gains a lot of sympathy, but later you can view the whole situation with a cold heart. We got so sick of it all we felt like swinging at some of them. That is because there is so much of it everywhere and besides, these people brought this upon themselves."*

Note: Bill had no way of knowing how much Allied bombing had devastated Naples, cutting the city off from the farming region so that the population had very little food and mass unemployment. The German occupiers in September,

1943, executed thousands of ordinary citizens, firing into lines of women waiting to buy bread, and further wasting the city. When the Germans withdrew, they destroyed the city's archives which, in effect, destroyed much of the city's history.

"The primitive horse carts are silhouetted against the Bay of Naples and Mt. Vesuvius."

"A crowded market place."

"This was taken in a dirty market place. Those are tiny fishes heaped on the table in the foreground. In the background is a butcher shop with a display of not very fresh meat outside. All the attention seems to be on the little boy who wears a very guilty expression."

"These people are painting wooden balls bright colors. I've seen them for sale in many shops, but to this day don't know what they are used for."

"On the way to the top of castle hill. The small steps and alley-ways are typical of those from the top to the bottom."

"Looking south from the castle hill, which is located in the center of the city."

The return trip to camp from Naples was much faster as Bill and his buddies *"hopped a ride on a B-17."*

By the middle of March 1945, the United States 1st Army had crossed the Rhine River and from the East the Russians were advancing towards Berlin. Bill observed:

> *"I believe that if Germany does not give up, including all of her industry along the Rhine, that the war will last for a long time yet. Then every last inch of Germany would have to be occupied and each individual German beaten. There can only be a lasting peace after the war if the men who have done the fighting are given a chance to say what is to be done with the conquered nations. Who else could possibly know more about the enemy? The peace terms must be harsh enough to show the people that war does not pay. Already the officials who sit in Washington and actually know very little of conditions over here have turned the Italian government over to these very men who were responsible for the war! You can't handle a conquered nation with kid gloves and not expect them to take advantage of you.... I'm sure that if enough men and women of our great country take an active interest in the present situation we must arrive at the correct solution."*

Note: The jurisdiction of part of southern Italy, Sicily and Sardinia was returned to the Italians in February, 1944, under the supervision of the Allied Military Government. A coalition cabinet was composed of six parties, some of whom had resisted Fascism, such as the Communists. Ivanhoe Bonomi, an anti-Fascist and a Reformist Socialist, was Premier from June 4, 1944, to June 17, 1945. King Victor Emanuelle, in spite of his collaboration with Mussolini and the Fascists for two decades, retained the monarchy until his abdication on May 9, 1946. His son, who succeeded him as King Umberto II, fled the country on June 13 after the Italians approved a referendum to abolish the monarchy and proclaim Italy a republic.

Bill enclosed a poem in one of his letters written by an Air Corps PFC and printed in one of the Army's publications such as *Stars and Stripes:*

> *Italy, Italy, Italy, to me it's all the same,*
> *Snow, heat and mountains, and a lot of rain,*
> *The climate is rotten and the women are worse,*
> *All the Ityes can do is to drain one's purse.*
>
> *The streets are dirty, the people the same,*
> *About all that's left of Italy is just a frame,*
> *The country is supposed to be beautiful, even Pompeii,*
> *But, pal, I'll tell you, I'm ready to call it a day.*
>
> *Please don't think this is to be a gripe or a groan,*
> *I just want to hurry, and get started home,*
> *Leave Italy to the Ityes, and GEORGIA to me,*
> *Then we'll all be happy, just you wait and see.*

These words expressed the average soldier's war-weariness, the despair with a ravaged country and its depressed people, and most of all, a longing to be done with war and go home.

In his March 27 letter Bill had some interesting observations about the status of women in Italy.

> "Here, especially in the central mountain regions, you'll find women who seem to be reduced to mere work animals. On one particular stop through we watched about ten women workers for a long time.

Their ages ran from about 15 to 65. Their clothes were extremely ragged and their feet were all bare. It was their job to transport huge piles of manure into the fields for fertilization. They carried it on their heads in huge baskets. The manure was loaded by two men, and it took both of them to lift a full basket on the woman's back. I was never aware that things like that still went on in this supposedly civilized country. It's not at all an uncommon sight to see women walking around town with huge bundles on their heads. Everyone to their own customs I guess, and they can have them."

The war, as Bill wrote on April 8, "keeps rolling on in our favor, but the stubborn German just keeps fighting on." In the Pacific the American Marines made advances, but slowly and at great costs. In early April the Marines invaded Okinawa, sank a Japanese battleship, two cruisers, and three destroyers. The battle for Okinawa would last for two bitter months, but by June 21, 1945, the Americans prevailed and established an air base only 325 miles from the Japanese homeland. But in April, Bill was most concerned about where he might be sent when the European war ended. He remarked:

"An announcement by General Marshall sort of struck me. It said that with the end of the European war quick moves to the CBI [China-Burma-India] theater can be expected; that is without first getting a furlough to the States."

Victory in Europe was imminent. Then the sudden death of President Roosevelt on April 12 shocked all Americans.

Roosevelt would not live to see the conclusion of a war to which he had dedicated the last four years of his life. Bill was quite moved by this news, and he wrote on April 14:

> *"Roosevelt had some very definite ideas and plans which he would have been able to successfully carry out. Most people voted for F.D.R. never realizing that Truman would be President so soon after the fourth term began. We have but one course to follow and that is to rally around the new President and give him all the support we can. I'm sure there are enough good men in the cabinet and both Houses to carry on as though nothing had happened."*

President Harry Truman, thrust into the office with very little knowledge of the Allies war strategy, would have many momentous decisions to make before the final surrender of the Axis countries.

The men in Italy were waiting in daily expectation of a German capitulation. For diversion Bill spent time with his little dog, Smudgepot:

> *"Just came back from a little walk with Smudgepot. There are a lot of lizards and she loves to catch them. They are too fast for her. When she does get one she plays with it as a cat would with a mouse. She is certainly the best source of entertainment over here for me."*

Besides playing with the dog, Bill and his comrades had many discussions about the future of America. One of the topics focused on postwar business:

> *"Most of the boys don't agree that they (Eastman Kodak) should be allowed to control retail stores such as the one you work for. Many of these boys hope some day to have small businesses of their own, so of course they feel that a company like that will hinder them by monopolizing a certain field. I'm sort of inclined to agree, for already they have bought out smaller concerns, and I know that after the war intend to open many more of their own stores. A small businessman could hardly compete with any company so large.*
>
> *I believe that each company should be required to stay within its own field be that what it may: manufacturing, retailing, wholesaling, etc. That would distribute power and always leave room for fair competition."*

Another topic which the boys discussed was the maintenance of a peacetime army:

> "I don't think we should adopt the Swiss plan [every male must serve a certain amount of time each year in service until the age of 55]. I don't want to see anyone spend any of their time in military training unless it is purely voluntary. I believe that if men who were willing to make the army their career were given a good deal many more would make the army their permanent job. A peacetime army should be run as a big concern and the men paid good wages. I'm sure that things can be worked out without subjecting every young man to army life for any period of time. I know that I wouldn't want my son to have anything to do with this army if it can possibly be avoided. [But] we must have a standing peacetime army and navy and must always be ready to mobilize the full strength of the nation."

Most of all, the boys discussed what they would do after returning home to a nation at peace. After spending three to five years of the prime years of their youth in the service of their country, many soldiers had no idea what they wanted to do or of what they were capable. As Bill remarked in his April 30 letter, *"Too many are dreaming of high paying jobs, beautiful cars, homes, etc. When you speak to these men actually very few know or have any idea as to how they are going to get all these things."* Bill was more realistic. He had thought many hours about his future:

> "Now that the end of all this war comes closer and closer you think more each day of just what will I do when I get out of the army. I'm quite sure that I would like some part of photography as my life's work.

So when I'm discharged the thing to do would be to take the best possible job available within that field and just learn everything possible, and, possibly even continue going to college at night. Then later, when I feel confident enough, open a business of my own."

One of the most positive effects of Bill's wartime service would be his personal discovery of photography as a creative art form which he would ever pursue.

As Bill mused about his future plans, the war in Europe came to a conclusion. German army divisions collapsed and surrendered throughout Germany and Italy. Mussolini, no longer protected by Germans, tried to flee to Switzerland but was captured and assassinated by Italian Partisans on April 28. Adolph Hitler, amid the final shelling of Berlin by the Russians, committed suicide in his bunker on April 30. Finally, German Army leaders signed the terms of unconditional surrender at Supreme Commander General Eisenhower's headquarters in Reims, France. V-E Day, Victory in Europe, was proclaimed on May 8, 1945.

V-E Day released all the pent-up tension that Americans had felt since the attack on Pearl Harbor. At last the Nazis were defeated! Celebrations erupted everywhere. I remember hearing the announcement in the evening when a neighbor and I were in a local drug store buying ice cream cones. I was thinking how Bill would enjoy this cone as he had written that fresh milk and ice cream were the two foods he missed the most. While we ate our cones, the radio proclaimed the news. My friend's husband was a German prisoner of war, and her elation was indescribable. Everyone in the store and those on the street shouted and screamed: the war is over! But, not yet. We still had the war in the Pacific which was fought desperately.

America prepared to fight the Japanese to a final victory. Thus began a massive redirection of American forces from Europe to the Pacific in preparation for an invasion of the Japanese homeland. An increased air offensive of bombers against the major cities in Japan firebombed and destroyed factories, homes, and killed many people. But still the Japanese were unwilling to surrender. The American soldiers in Europe, the ones who were left in Italy, France, Germany, waited and wondered where and when they would be sent.

Bill wrote on May 12: *"You know we're all back in the same old spot, just wondering what will happen next."* The Army had announced a point system, effective on V-E Day, which would determine the order of demobilization of the troops. Bill was concerned because as he remarked humorously:

> *"I'm afraid that I've been caught with my points down."*

However, Bill did not think that the point system would

affect him as his type of technology would be needed in the Japanese campaign still in progress. Despite his misgivings, he was optimistic that the war would end soon:

> "I'm of the opinion that Japan won't last very much longer. Her fleet of large battle wagons has been reduced to about three dozen, she has but about 8000 planes and an army of only 4,000,000. To me those figures point to an early victory for us. Now that Germany has accepted unconditional surrender Japan knows that the plan of the Axis to conquer the whole of the civilized world can never be realized."

The boys in San Severo began a period of waiting. The planes kept flying, for practice, not for bombing the Germans or photographing enemy installations. Bill recounted an amusing, but quite frightening, incident:

> "While a Spitfire [British fighter plane] taxis there is always a man sitting on the wing and another on the tail to avoid it tipping over. Somehow this Spitfire took off with the man still on the tail. It wasn't till the plane had gone out about five miles when they radioed the pilot and told him of his cargo. When he landed the man on the tail was unhurt. That must have been quite an experience. Bet he won't care to do much flying after that."

With very little for the men to do, the Squadron arranged for trucks to transport groups of men to the beaches on the Adriatic Sea about fifty miles from San Severo. Each man was privileged to take two trips a week in addition to some arranged sight-seeing trips to nearby villages.

"Looking East towards the Adriatic Sea from San Severo, Italy, June 1945"

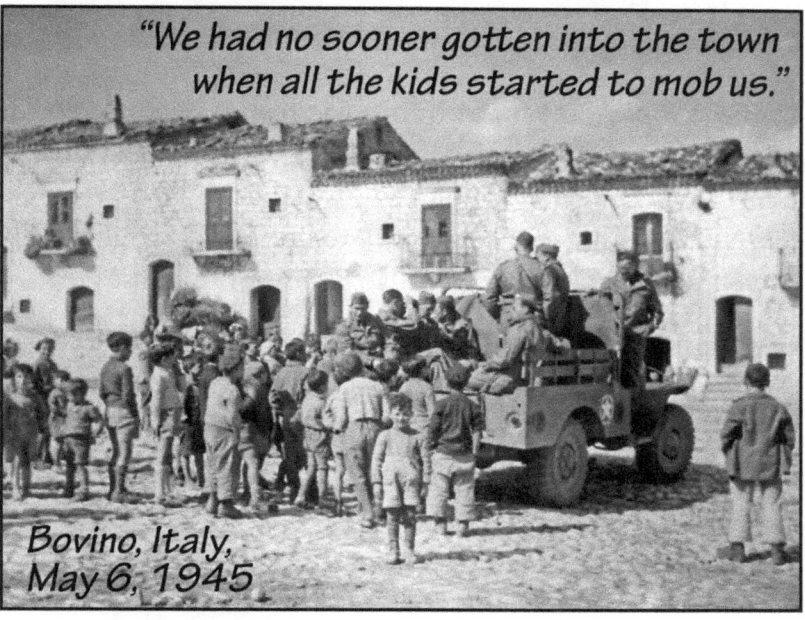

"We had no sooner gotten into the town when all the kids started to mob us."

Bovino, Italy, May 6, 1945

Bill took his dog, Smudgepot, along and let her swim, too, and chase thrown bamboo sticks.

Smudge Pot swimming at Lake Lessina, near the Adriatic Sea May, 1945

This was a pleasant interim, but the reality of war crept in, and the Squadron began to pack up the photo laboratory.

The laboratory was located in a barn. Now that the censorship was lifted, Bill could describe his arrival in Italy, November, 1944, and the construction of the base.

> "When we first landed in Naples we went to a reception center. After spending only two days there, I left as a part of the advanced detail. We flew from Naples up to Leghorn. From Leghorn we drove back to Naples with all the equipment we had picked up at Leghorn. From Naples we flew here to San Severo in a B-24. When we first got here this olive grove, where our camp now stands, was just an empty place with about a foot or more of mud. For about a month we

> *lived in a billet in town coming out here each day to work on setting up the camp. We hauled up all the tents and set them in their proper places. We built a mess hall with tables and a cement floor. Then built latrines, roads, etc. Building a place which will serve a squadron of men as large as this is quite a problem.*
>
> *Our laboratory was set up in an old barn. Upon arrival it was smelly, had a cobblestone floor and the roof leaked pretty bad. We proceeded to put in a brick floor getting a few at a time from broken down houses. Then we started unpacking and as we did that we built rooms and partitions from the wood which we got from the crates. For water we put a pump and filtering system into an old well near by. In an extremely short while we flew our first mission."*

Now everything was coming down, but still no word whether the Squadron would be shipping out soon.

Boredom was setting in for many of the soldiers, and some took on a very dangerous activity:

> *Some of the boys in our outfit were unfortunate enough to be picked up for doing business with the black market gang here in Italy. I must say that it is really quite a temptation once in a while to sell things at such a handsome profit; however, a man shouldn't do it if he knows of the heavy jail sentences being passed out. It's beyond me why a fellow would take a chance of selling something and then being caught and spending a number of years in jail. Of course, the fellows that were caught probably planned on making thousands of dollars.*

"Here is where I work. 37th Photo Reconnaissance Squadron."

San Severo, Italy, March 1945

Bill lamented the uncertainty of the Squadron's status and noted in his letter of May 23, 1945:

> *"While the war was still in progress huge formations of bombers used to pass overhead with their loads of bombs for the Germans. That is still the story: however now they travel the other way and instead of bombs they carry men of the Fifth Army who are headed back to the States. What a wonderful feeling it must be to know that at last you're really headed home."*

Heading home, though Bill's major focus, also meant parting with the dog that he and his friend, Bill Groethe, had become so fond. In early June, the Squadron decided to eliminate all the dogs, especially females, that the soldiers had adopted (which was against regulations). So the two Bills took Smudgepot to the nearby town to have a veterinarian spay her, but there were no vets. While they were gone, the Squadron rounded up a lot of dogs and shot them, so Smudgepot managed to avoid execution. Bill persuaded the Squadron doctor to spay the dog, but as Bill observed:

> *"We won't be able to take Smudge with us anyway. We'll have to try and find a nice native family who will take her."*

Bill inquired about permission to take Smudgepot home with him, providing he was destined to be sent to the States, but that was against regulations. Fortunately, the family in town who did his laundry agreed to take her when Bill finally shipped out.

Bill and Smudge Pot

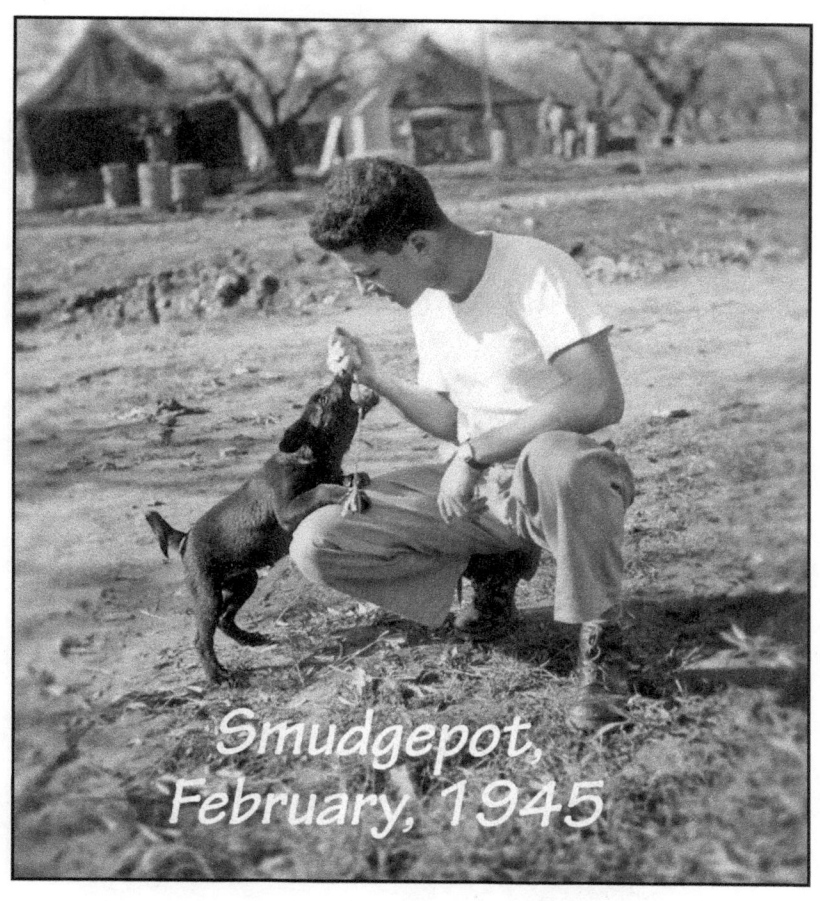

Our girl "Smudge Pot," April, 1945

Writing on June 14, Bill despaired that *"as well as you can see, we're all still sweating this thing out."* The days passed, and no orders came through. Bill spent the time talking to some of the local people and he described the plight of the farmer:

> "These people that work on the farms around here work extremely long hours. I always see them pull up with their donkey carts about six in the morning and they work from then until about 6 or 7 at night. It takes them an hour out from town and an hour back at night. One of the boys told me he makes only forty lire a day which is equivalent to forty cents in the States. Besides that the wealthy owner of the farm gives him enough flour to bake bread. He has a wife and five children. It's not hard to understand why most of these poor laborers are in rags when the price of a very poor pair of shoes is about thirty dollars. A new pair of shoes must be beyond their wildest dreams. Even though they are in rags and have to live worse than most animals, they'll beg you to sell them a pack of cigarettes for $1.50. It sounds strange, but that's the way these people are."

Days passed, and Bill managed to be awarded a furlough. His next letter dated June 30 was sent from the Isle of Capri where he would spend a week with his friend, Bill Groethe. Bill luxuriated in the "nice clean room."

> "It's great to be able to sleep on a soft bed with sheets. The food is good but it's hard to get enough of it. There is a place around the corner where you can get malted milks, sundaes, cokes and ice cream sodas. I thought I could put away much more ice cream than I did. Only four plates.
>
> We headed up the mountain from our hotel until we got to the other side of the island. The view is really magnificent. While walking on paths built right on

the side of a rock cliff one can't help but think about the work that was put in. The other day we noticed about ten women laborers. They carry 100 pound bags of cement up the mountain on their heads. A few of the women seemed to be 60 or 70 years old. I noticed one woman probably paying the rest off. She gave them 45 lire which is the same as 45 cents.

One afternoon we walked up to the castle of Tiberius. It's the highest point on the Island. Some very pretty homes are passed on the way up. These people certainly don't trust each other. All the houses have eight or ten foot walls around them, and usually there is chipped glass cemented on top of barbed wire.

One day we hired an Italian with a boat. We went to see the Blue Grotto Cave. I agree that it is the most beautiful sight on the whole Isle. From the outside the cave is only about four and a half feet wide and about that high. A rowboat can just go inside. The inside is monstrous. Once your eyes become accustomed to the different light you begin to appreciate the beauty. The whole of the water or an object placed in it turns the most enchanting blue. When we got out of the cave the sails were hoisted and sailing away we went. We went about half ways to Naples and then along the coast of Sorrento, another island right next to Capri."

On The Isle of Capri, May 1945

The rest leave ended, and the two Bills returned to camp.

The Squadron still had no word about orders. The men were kept busy with swimming trips, athletic games, and classes in math and English. Bill was still hopeful that the war in the Pacific would end soon, but he wrote on July 28, 1945.

> *"This period of waiting after the war [in Europe] has been won is definitely harder than war time operations itself. I'm just not going to make any more plans, predictions, or even get my hopes up. Everything always just goes haywire anyway."*

Many of the men in the Squadron were slated to serve in the occupation forces, and Bill was concerned that he might be one of those. He thought he would prefer going to the Pacific, providing he had a furlough in the States first, than spending endless more months in Italy as part of the occupation. But it was the uncertainty and daily boredom that made the days stretch endlessly.

The days seemed endless on the home front, too. Some of the infantrymen from the European theater began to return home, some permanently, some on their way to the Pacific. As I worked at Eastman Kodak's film counter, I viewed many of the photographs which these men deposited for development and printing. They were shocking! For the first time, the extent of the horror of Nazi concentration camps was encountered by the liberating forces. The pictures of emaciated bodies, thrown on piles like garbage by the retreating Germans, and the surviving skeletons of incarcerated prisoners brought the reality of Germany's genocide, soon to be termed the Holocaust, to every American. The Allies—Britain, the Soviet Union, the United States—had known of the exterminations of Jews by the Germans, but the extent of the operations were not acknowledged until December, 1942. A publication of the Polish Government-in-Exile in London entitled *The Mass Extermination of Jews in German-Occupied Poland* was printed in British newspapers and followed by a "declaration of solemn protest" by the three Allied Powers. But nothing further was done. Not until the Russians and the Americans approached camp after camp from the fall of 1944 to the spring of 1945 did the public become aware of the magnitude of Hitler's "Final Solution."

As the American public wondered in early August how long the Japanese would continue fighting, an awesome new weapon, an atomic bomb, was dropped on Hiroshima on August 6, 1945. This secret weapon, one that the Americans had developed over the past four years, had the force to obliterate a city and its people, expelling a deadly mushroom cloud of radioactive fallout. More importantly, using this weapon had unleashed a discussion which persists to this day: Was dropping The Bomb an immoral act? Could we have won the war without The Bomb? Were the Japanese about to surrender anyway? Reviewing the events prior to the decision to drop The Bomb and the war situation at that precise point in time will help to put this event in perspective.

All-out war requires all-out effort to destroy the enemy. With the possibility of developing a bomb that could take out a whole city, the Americans proceeded with the research whether or not it would ever be used. Intelligence suggested that the Russians were also working on such a bomb. The

Germans already had their V-1 unmanned flying bombs and then their V-2 rockets which they aimed at England, and, their scientists too, were trying to develop an atomic bomb. President Roosevelt and a close group of aides monitored the development of The Bomb, but when Roosevelt died, and Harry Truman succeeded him, there was a gap in communications. Vice-President Truman was never told about The Bomb. As President, Truman had no awareness of the existence of an atomic bomb until Secretary of War, Harry Stimson, advised him on April 25, 1945.

As yet, The Bomb had not been tested. A committee was formed of civilians including three scientists who had worked on the research with Secretary Stimson as chairman. Four physicists joined the panel and they included Robert Oppenheimer, head of the laboratory where the bomb was being assembled, and Enrico Fermi, responsible for developing the first steps of nuclear reaction at the University of Chicago. After much deliberation, the committee came to three conclusions:

- The bomb should be used on Japan as soon as possible.
- It should be used against war plants surrounded by workers' homes.
- It should be used without warning. [There was concern that a warning would allow the Japanese to bring American prisoners of war to the bomb site.]

When the results were brought to President Truman, he concurred, but he did not give the final approval. Indeed as Secretary Stimson warned, this awful weapon "might be the doom of civilization." On the other hand, the Japanese had refused to surrender and were preparing to defend the homeland after their desperate defense of Okinawa. Hundreds of kamikaze suicide bombers sank 30 U.S. ships; Japanese troops fought from caves. 12,000 Americans died, 36,000 were wounded, 110,000 Japanese died, and one third of the Okinawans were killed. Moreover, U.S. intelligence reported that the Japanese were preparing for the expected American invasion by recruiting every male from age 15 to 60 and every female from 17 to 45. They were being armed with every available weapon such as bamboo spears and even carpenter's awls. This fight to the death could cost a quarter of a million American lives, according to General George Marshall, and the war could last another year. With this information to consider, President Truman left for the Potsdam Conference in Prussia to meet with Stalin and Churchill.

On July 21 Truman received word in Potsdam that the testing of The Bomb had been successfully achieved in New Mexico. He conferred with Generals Marshall and Arnold, Admiral Leahy and his Secretary of Defense, Stimson. All agreed that The Bomb should be dropped on Japan even though as Truman wrote later, "I did not like the weapon." A warning message was prepared for the Japanese, to be termed the Potsdam Declaration, for delivery on July 27. The Declaration assured the Japanese that surrender would not mean that they would "be enslaved as a race or destroyed as a nation." The only alternative to unconditional surrender of the armed forces was "prompt and utter destruction" thus alluding to The Bomb without defining it. Leaflets with a printed translation of the Declaration were dropped on Japanese cities by American bombers throughout the day. Officially, the Japanese Prime Minister Kautaro Suzuki ignored the threat as "nothing but a rehash of old proposals." With this information, Truman made his final decision. On July 31 he sent the message to the War Department: "Release when ready but not sooner than August 2." The Potsdam Conference would then be concluded and Truman would be en route to the United States.

The Bomb was dropped on Hiroshima on August 6, 1945. Approximately 80,000 people died instantly, 50,000 to 60,000 died within a few months, countless others and future generations would suffer from radiation sickness or birth defects for years to come. President Truman waited, but no sign of surrender was forthcoming. On August 9 Japan's Supreme Council for the Direction of the War met in Prime Minister Suzuki's bomb shelter to debate the next course of action. Two generals and one admiral refused surrender and claimed that this was the time to lure the Americans ashore. The War Minister, General Anami, insisted that national honor required one last great battle on Japanese soil: "Would it not be wondrous for the whole nation to be destroyed like a beautiful flower?" The news was brought in that a second bomb had fallen on Nagasaki killing 70,000 people. At the same time, the Soviet Union declared war on Japan and invaded Manchuria. The meeting adjourned, and that night Emperor Hirohito made the decision that Japan must surrender.

Japan surrendered on August 14, 1945. The war was over amid glorious celebrations all over the United States. Generations may debate the morality of unleashing the atomic bomb and commencing the nuclear age. However, the arms race with intercontinental ballistic missiles containing nuclear warheads which Russia and the United States aimed at each other in the 1950's and 1960's defined a cold war which was made not by nuclear blasts, but by the results of world conflict and aggression. President Truman and his Cabinet, faced with mounting American casualties and a war weary nation in 1945, made a choice which ended the war far sooner with less American lives than if we had invaded Japan. Whether the United States had used the bomb or not, eventually nuclear weapons would have been developed by other countries. As early as 1942 the Russians had begun developing nuclear energy, helped by the information secretly transmitted to them by the German-born, British naturalized, physicist, Klaus Fuchs, who was a part of American atomic research at Los Alamos, New Mexico. The discovery and use of nuclear energy was as inevitable as the discovery of electricity.

I had not heard from Bill for a month, so I surmised that he had shipped out of Italy, but to where? Then a letter arrived, dated August 19:

> *"I've been slated to go straight for the Pacific. I'm writing this from the American Red Cross in Naples. We're stationed in an old volcano right outside the city limits. Being here just as peace came may turn out to be a wonderful break for our squadron. If things go as they are supposed to right now I should be in the States in three weeks or so."*

The next communication was a telegram from Camp Shanks, New York on September 9:

> *"Barb dear arrived in New York today."*

The moment we had waited for so long had arrived: Peace and the return of the troops.

In his next letter Bill described the experience of arriving in New York harbor:

> *"Our ship, the* Sea Scamp, *pulled into New York just last Wednesday. What a thrill seeing the old familiar skyline once again! I tried getting a call through to*

you, but I guess you can imagine what it's like having fourteen thousand men from the Queen Elizabeth *and three thousand from the* Sea Scamp *all rush for a telephone booth.*

I just can't wait to see you now that I'm home, however I think it's best that I get myself straightened out here before going elsewhere."

Leaving Naples Bay, Italy
August, 1945

The Ride Home on the Sea Scamp

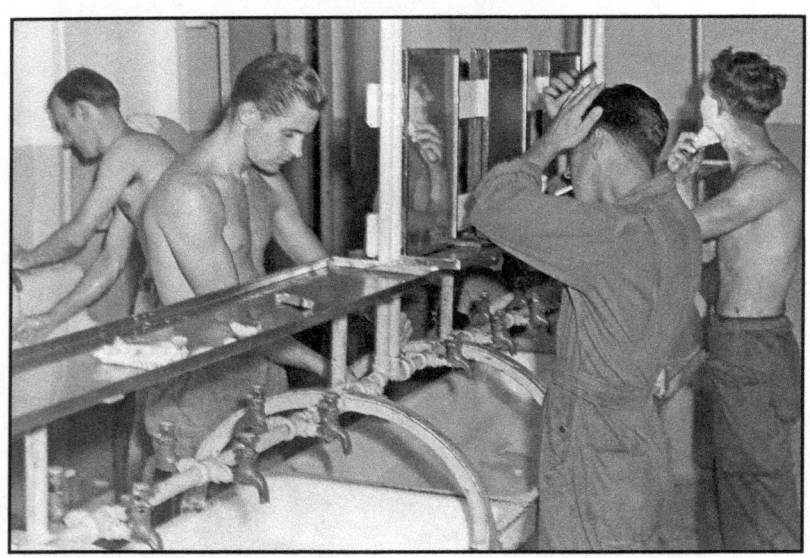

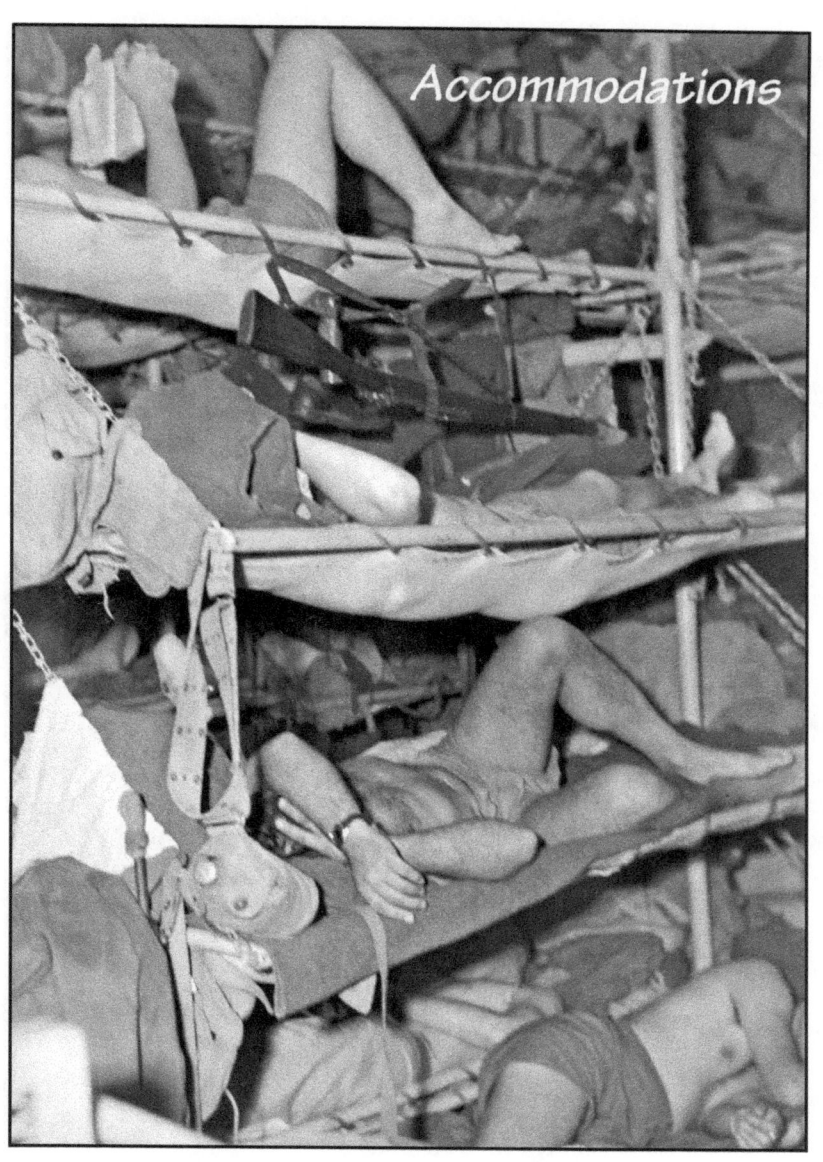

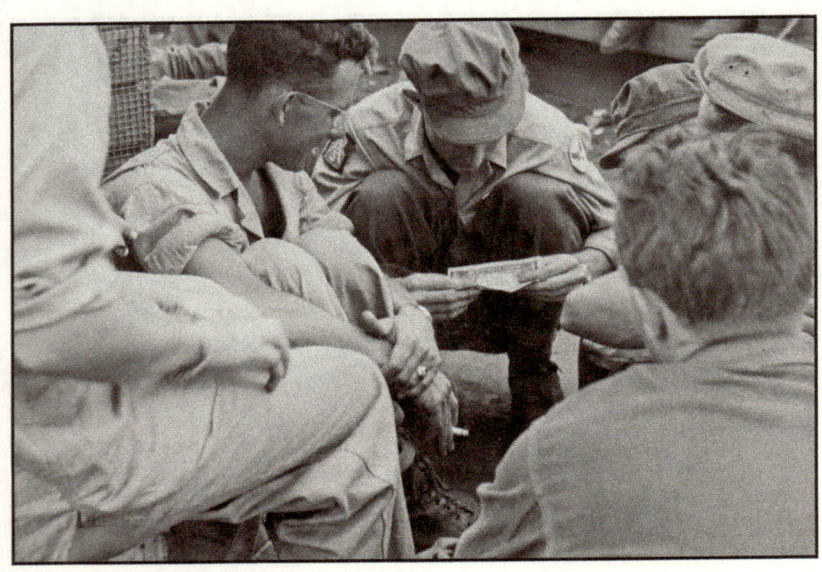

Within a week Bill had his affairs in order, a railroad ticket purchased, and he arrived in Chicago on September 22.

We had two weeks together. This was our first opportunity to get acquainted face to face since our brief meeting in the fall of 1944. My parents made room for him in our small house in Palatine, and our time was spent visiting the city, taking long walks and just having fun. We became engaged, officially, and agreed to get married as soon as Bill was discharged. With so many men returning from both military theaters, the discharge camps were overwhelmed. As a result, Bill received extension after extension of leave, so he could not make any definite plans.

Cook County Illinois, 1945...

...Picnic at Deer Grove Forest Preserve

When Bill returned to New Jersey, he filled the time with small repairs around his parents' home in Union. He built an enlarger and a printer so that he could develop and print his films. He wrote on October 10:

> *"My thoughts are with you always. Barb, darling, things won't be easy for us probably for a long time."*

Things were not easy, and the next few months were perhaps one of the most difficult times of our lives together.

After three years of being ordered what to do and where to go, Bill was suddenly faced with the need to find a job upon discharge, locate an apartment for us, plan ahead for attending college, and have enough money to get started. Bill started exploring the college situation first, and as he had already contacted the University of Michigan, they responded by assuring him that he would probably be admitted for the fall, 1946, term providing his transcript from his pre-war year at Cooper Union's evening school was satisfactory. On the other hand Cooper Union would save a place for him, also for the fall term, 1946, continuing the scholarship which he had held prior to induction into the Army. Bill knew for certain that he wanted to pursue a career in art, and he aspired to be an art director "which is a very good paying job, anywhere from $5000 to $50,000 a year."

Housing, especially furnished apartments, was practically non-existent with so many returning service men looking for identical quarters. Bill looked around the New York-New Jersey area, but there was nothing. The most immediate need, a job after discharge, was even more elusive. Bill went to an employment agency, and he described the situation:

> "The place was jammed. When finally I was interviewed I found they had nothing at all in my line. I did file a claim for unemployment compensation. If I'm not employed by next Friday I can collect $20. The place was just overflowing with ex-service men collecting unemployment insurance. Most of them are pretty disgusted and ready to start a war against civilians. Can't really blame them. After being away living a tough life for so long, they at least expect the right to work for a living wage upon discharge."

Long before the war ended, the Government had anticipated the problems that the country would face with so many men returning home. The years after World War I had been full of turmoil, and unemployed veterans had set up a tent city in Washington, D.C., demanding a bonus in the midst of the worst depression the country had ever seen. The situation after World War II promised to be even more fraught with conflict, with many more veterans returning, so in order to provide opportunities, and to prevent civilian upheaval, the G.I. Bill was passed. This allowed every veteran to obtain an education, if desired, with government support. Discharged veterans could receive $20 unemployment insurance for 52 weeks, if needed, although most veterans either chose to attend college or found employment. The Bill also provided for guaranteed low-interest mortgages which stimulated the development of mass housing for veterans and their families in the decade after the war's end.

The G.I. Bill changed a whole generation. It enabled the expansion of colleges and universities, encouraged research and provided advanced education to men who would never have had the opportunity before the war. And, importantly, for civil society, it provided an occupation for the men until the war industry gradually converted to a peace time economy. The tremendous growth of the U.S. economy in the second half of the century owes much to the educated generation of World War II veterans, such as Bill Farr.

With his college future decided—Cooper Union in the fall, 1946— and his financial situation fairly solvent "$100 in the bank and $300 in bonds," Bill waited and waited for his discharge. As the leave extensions continued, I decided to take a trip to New Jersey, meet Bill's family, and spend some time together. This plan created an upheaval between us and nearly derailed our engagement.

In response to my letter in mid-October suggesting my visit, Bill sent a telegram:

"*Stay where you are. Will write later.*"

My parents, who were against my taking the trip in the first place, said, "See, he must have something to hide." They liked Bill, enjoyed his stay with us and approved of him, but they were adamant that we should not get married yet. Understandably, parents are reluctant for their eighteen year old only child to marry someone from across the country, and with foreign-born parents, too! If the war had not occurred, I would have married a mid-western home town boy and lived somewhere down the street. But the war changed everything.

Bill had nothing to hide. He was just overly conscious about his modest home:

> *"My parents felt so very bad not being able to offer you a nice place to stay if you cared to visit. My sister Rita cried when I told her you wanted to come and that I wired you not to. It just isn't possible for you to stay here. The house is built so that it is almost impossible to house guests. Here you would encounter many inconveniences which I would not have you do. I can only hope that you will understand."*

I didn't! After not receiving any more letters from me, Bill had second thoughts. He telephoned on October 18, followed by a letter:

> *"Just knowing you're coming makes me so very happy. The family is so very enthused about it, too. I'm sure that they'll make it as comfortable as possible."*

And they did. My trip by overnight coach train to Newark, New Jersey, was an exciting experience. I had never been out of the state of Illinois, and the thrill of passing through the states between Illinois and the East Coast was overwhelming. Bill's family welcomed me warmly, and their accommodations were quite satisfactory. After all, I was not accustomed to the Waldorf-Astoria! In fact, my first glimpse of New York City, from the Hoboken ferry boat, was unforgettable. The visit to the Farr family was most positive, but Bill was still not discharged. He had no information when he might be called to Fort Dix, so after a two week visit, I returned home on the all-coach Pennsylvania Railroad's "Trail Blazer."

Barb visits Union, New Jersey, USA October, 1945

Several weeks later, Bill was called to Fort Dix for a week of "mustering out," and, officially, on November 23 Staff

Sergeant William Farr, Number 32760534, was discharged. He wrote:

"Tonight I am the civilian that I've dreamed about being so long. It's a grand feeling."

For his discharge, Bill received $223.57, $60 allotment for November, $200 mustering out pay and six $10 war bonds.

The next day Bill went shopping to buy his first civilian clothes. He bought a suit for $55 and an overcoat for $39.50. He deplored the inflation as he had to pay $3.98 for a shirt which was only 79 cents before the war. A new pair of shoes cost $4.95. Bill was ready to put army life behind him and face the future as a civilian.

The postwar world was not the glorious peace that everyone had envisioned. It was inevitable that the veterans, who had viewed coming home with euphoria, would be disappointed and frustrated. Moreover, the world situation was far from peaceful. Bill listened to the news reports, and wrote his feelings, which, no doubt, were shared by many ex-soldiers:

"December 2, 1945

Sometimes a person can get quite depressed just listening to a few news reports and reading a paper. The so called leaders have certainly brought the world into a pretty rotten position. The most destructive war the world has ever seen is finished and already the Germans are about to rebel again, the far eastern situation is such that with a wrong move we might get into a war with Russia because of interference in the Chinese Civil War, Britain demands a portion of the atomic bombs already manufactured [actually,

> *the U.S. had only one bomb left]; why, if she doesn't intend to use them?*
>
> *Worst of all, the veterans of these United States get pushed around in the country they fought for, they can't find homes or jobs."*

With scarce jobs and little available housing in the New York-New Jersey area, and Bill's plans to enter Cooper Union in the fall of 1946, we decided that his coming to Chicago would be the best immediate course of action. He wrote his last letter on December 17 advising that he would be arriving in Chicago on Thursday, December 20. As ever, Bill was optimistic about the future:

> *"I realize that ordinarily people don't get married and then head for college. Ordinarily men don't give up three of the best years of their life either. We are very fortunate for we are young. Thousands of people, older than we, are doing what we intend to do."*

Christmas, 1945, our first together, was a happy time. Shortly after the New Year, Bill obtained a job with Oscar and Associates, a photography studio, and began to learn the process of commercial photography. We were married on February 2, 1946.

The war defined our lives. We spent our childhoods growing up in the midst of a national economic depression. Unemployment reached extraordinary levels and many Americans had little to eat or adequate shelter. "Hobos"—the homeless—riding the rails of freight trains were a common sight. Most of us were poor. Just as the nation began to experience some prosperity, the war commenced and America's young men were sent to the battlefields of Europe, Africa and Asia.

Bill was one of those young men who fought the "war to save democracy." And, like other returning service men, he went to college, he started a family, he bought a house on the G.I. Bill for 5% down and a 4½% mortgage, and he helped to shape the post-war world. These letters are a testament to the experiences of an American soldier in World War II and his hopes and dreams. As such, the letters form an important historical document in the mosaic of war experiences, but they also define an individual of high integrity who cared for his country, cared for people and eloquently expressed his deepest feelings. These letters tell the story of World War II, but, most importantly, they tell the story of a romance.

Mon. Eve August 20, 1949

My Darling;

    Wonder if I miss you? — I
miss you as the sky would stars
   whose everlasting rays
   bring hope to nights engulfing loneliness.
Loneliness,
   prolonged loneliness.
   Oars to bear,
   while clouds between hold back —
   Love,
   Devotion,
We sense God's hand
   guiding the winds,
   breaking darkened clouds
   till atmosphere
   is in gem-like splendor veiled.
Could that our love through parting
   find the fragrant freshness
   left by parting rain?
Love;
   Richer,
     Deeper,
      Clearer than before.

Miss you?
  Will kiss you
   as the budding rose the sun.
Morn is come,
  gripping love its warmth unfold.
The night will fall again,
  Cloudless.

Barbara Storm Farr as you may suspect from reading this book, is an accomplished researcher, writer, and historian.

She was awarded a Bachelor of Arts, Roosevelt University, Master of Arts and Doctor of Philosophy in History, the University of Illinois at Chicago, has published many articles and a book on "The Development and Impact of Right Wing Politics in Britain, 1903–1932" (Garland Publishing, Inc., New York, London 1987)

As a member of the League of Women Voters of Moore County, NC, she has researched and produced Special Reports on Children at Risk and A Portrait of Poverty in Moore County, North Carolina.

A special message from the publisher...

Thanks for your interest in *A History of World War Two Told in Letters, Stories of Romance, and Vintage Photos*. I hope you enjoyed the journey!

I also hope that if you liked this book, you'll help us "spread the word" by letting others know about it, and by leaving us a nice review on Amazon or any of the other book review sites. We would really appreciate it!

For all other comments and contacts you can send us a message via the contact form at *www.obepub.com*.

Other books from Old Barn Publishing

How to Canoe in Canada, almost get killed by rapids, eaten by polar bears, have your blood sucked out by clouds of mosquitoes, and other fun stuff by Jeff Farr

The Awakening of Surry County by Tom Scheve

For additional titles, book descriptions, purchase options, and to subscribe to receive updates, early notifications and special offers, visit obepub.com

Do *you* have a story to tell?

Visit us at obepub.com to learn how you can get your stories into e-book and print formats. Today's technology makes it both practical and economical even if your audience is just family and friends (if it's larger, we may end sending you some nice royalty checks!). In any case, don't let your stories and experiences get lost. Books — *both electronic and printed* — are the perfect way to preserve information for future generations... and a fun and rewarding project for *you*, the author! **Check out the possibilities at obepub.com.**

www.ingramcontent.com/pod-product-compliance
Lightning Source LLC
LaVergne TN
LVHW011422080426
835512LV00005B/209